#TakesCourage

Psalm 31:24 MSG
"Be brave. Be strong. Don't give up.
Expect GOD to get here soon."

B.Leah

iambleah1@gmail.com or *(508) 622-5324*

ISBN:1511581611
ISBN-13:9781511581615

7/10/15

Megan,
Thank you for being
a gem that is precious +
genuine. WRITED N
SISTER!

DEDICATION

This is for you. And me.

It #TakesCourage
to follow The
Lord in all
your ways!

♡ B. Leah

Thank
you

CONTENTS

Jesus, is my goal and hope everywhere I go.
Grateful for my gifted, intentional, and prayerful husband Ché. And my
children that never get enough of me no matter how many times my words
or eyes didn't nurture them. I learned the way I should go from Kenric
(dad) & Deborah (mom). I am grateful for family, friends and colleagues
that loved me long, hard, and strangely enough to help me give birth to
poetry that "Speaks Truth to Power". To the number of individuals and
families struggling with the impact of oppression I see you. I hope, watch,
fight, and pray for justice for and with you. Special appreciation to
Annmarie G. Sirotnak of AG Design
http://www.agdesigngraphics.com/ and **Elijah Hooker of Captured by
Elijah** http://www.capturedbyelijah.com/ Annmarie is responsible for
the cover artwork and promotional material used for "Takes Courage".
Elijah is responsible for photographs (back cover of book and page 40). I
am so grateful for God's gifts and spirit of excellence in you Annmarie &
Elijah. Thank you Kate Foran & Tarishi M.I.D.N.I.G.H.T. Shuler for helping
to edit "Takes Courage". #shewrites small group, y'all are like doulas;
God bless you Crystal Senter Brown, Darlene "MaPeach Productions"
Brandon & Lynnette Johnson.

I acknowledge that God made us in His image.
I acknowledge that the sun rises and sets without my needing to worry.
I acknowledge that I do not know it all.
I acknowledge that I have clipped others wings. I apologize.
I acknowledge that I have shown up to work late.
*I acknowledge that there are countless men, women, and children who've
been neglected, abused, and sexually violated. I acknowledge that it
was/is NOT your fault! I acknowledge that there is more after this.*

"The world is in desperate need of healing and direction. The words from this poet are a salve and a compass. This is a work of art, heart and faith. God gifted Leah with a desire to write and she has developed a remarkable skill. Her pen is anointed. We were waiting for this. "

Lynnette Elizabeth Johnson -Author of "I've Been Meaning to Tell You" https://www.facebook.com/ellejaefan

"In a world that can sometimes be dark, Leah is a shining example of God's light! She is gifted in the art of true devotion, and this evident in her writing and performances. She doesn't just talk the talk, she uses her LIFE to walk the walk. I am thrilled that she has decided to share her newest poetry collection with us because it will allow us to have a small piece of her light and encouragement to carry around with us each and every day. Shine on, sister!"

Crystal Senter-Brown
Mama, Wife, Poet, Author, Teacher
http://crystalsenterbrown.weebly.com/

"Leah is the poet while existing as poetry. She is a journey, turned testimony, gathered into stanzas. The woman you meet in her art is identical to the one who will pray with you in your living room on a Tuesday afternoon. That is why her poetry is captivating, her authenticity resounds from the page and finds its way into your spirit. I have no doubt that God adds a blessing to the reading of these words."

Shanna Tanika Melton, Poet, Recording Artist, Painter, Educator
http://shatamel.wix.com/poeticsoularts-net

AUDIENCE OF ONE

and i am not sure what she will say
about the notes - belting out E-Flats in heels with no
pantyhose
she abstains from coffee & veal
her hips tell a different story. no more bumping and grinding
cut that out the diet along with deceit & envy
standing 5 feet whatever. eyes closed. head at snooze.
this is about who is listening
when you're texting your boo & looking for condoms & lip
gloss

i remember ONE night,
they were just friends until he & she became we
sworn to discretion
no phone calls. only postage. unpaid.
ONE too many drinks, one mourning. In bed. one lie after the
next
chips & ice cream never cured the sadness - it just made her
fat.

i heard the cries for help. after hair being pulled
hand meeting face. red. burning with insecurity.
blood melting the sidewalks
& there ain't enough bleach. vampires were here.
slinging crack. penetrating families with bullets and
prostitution and tasers
they are the goliaths. searching for crowns after each
conquest.

while i dreamed in world tours & fast cars
thousands of heartbeats resting on sleeves
driving gloves, stadium lights & this band
i know very little about musicianship
but i know sound.

He delivered me from looking for compliments
validation & approval. i used to hope for applause

until His hands holding me together became enough
He picks me out of the trash. Rescues us from heaps of litter
He prefers us close. till' our steps become His
opening His mouth & the sweetest aroma fills the room
i want to want you ONLY
i want to climb mountains and at the highest peak
Father You show us greater
i want His breath on my face
in the morning.

Use the space below to write your thoughts.
Write about your 1st kiss.

MOTHERS DAY

I remember thinking about motherhood
But not ever really having concrete plans to.
Then BAM
Missed period. Test positive.
I remember not knowing what it would be like
But knowing it would be alright.
I remember the sweet scent on each of my their necks
Wished I could soak a sponge and ring it out now and later.

I remember my body carrying one baby
Tucked neatly and she rested there until they said it was
time
I remember my body carrying another life
Tucked neatly and it rested there until i said it was time
I remember my body carrying two babies
Tucked neatly and they played there until they said it was
time
 Have you ever carried
      water
      and placenta
      and membranes
      and muscles
      and other heart beats
      and limbs
      and love
      and dreams
      and hope
      and God's purpose for other people
Across state lines,
On an air craft,
On a double-decker train,
While riding in cars with boys,
To the altar or everyday to work?
I know mothers
that stand tall, wide, short, bronzed, silver, patient, and truth
telling
mothers that go without eating

knitting new socks, jerking chicken, scrambling tofu
praying before speaking, dressed in love
forgiving over and over and over again
I know mothers
dentures replace teeth
crowned and she is the jewel of God's eye
I know mothers guilty as charged
doing life sentences In kitchens
on her knees scrubbing
wiping cheerios from ceilings
loving her children till death parts her

I know mothers whose children didn't survive
taken on street corners or at birth
counting her blessings
releasing her first fruit, harvesting hope
faith is her secret, love is her prize
she walks hours, her soles be going home
as her soul be longing for more
Christ in the storm, more joy beyond belief

I know mothers & wives hoping to be mothers
and sisters desiring to be mothers
and daughters learning how to be mothers
I know mothers that cry before they smile
searching for scriptures to explain the sorrow

I know mothers
beautiful, sweet, and humble
mothers that Let God. one day at a time
I know mothers
combing, brushing, and bathing everyone else
ironing and washing, folding and polishing
mothers who take their time
mothers' driving until the destination is reached
stirring and encouraging, empowering and baking
declaring victory on battle fields
I KNOW MOTHERS!

©2015 Ché Burgess
"Two of Three"
Greenbelt, Maryland 2015

Use the space below to write your thoughts.
Write about mothers that can't see their children.

PRETTY ONE

When you blot your lips and bat your eyes

Do you remember calves? Golden?

Relationships weren't enough

So collecting lip gloss became our fancy

 want to see you in the morning

Before you know you've arrived

Before the dew on tulips

Before the before

I want you to see you then

So I can encourage you to rest.

|.|

everything changed
and stayed the same
we use her to end thoughts
and begin anew

she got it and i mourned
the days of her being empty handed
no baggage, no chance of swimming
without equipment or a calendar
i cried.
wanted to tell Eve about herself
there she was in Eden, drenched in perfection
miracle after miracle. but she made it scary
no explanation, no womanly talks
it was nonchalant & careless
then i remembered
healing, the truth, the purity, her beauty, she's still there
at 10 & 12 & 13 & 8th grade will never be the same

she & time tell each other secrets
always with her in mind
like "she's beautiful - when will she find out"

she thought she could get pregnant all by herself
thought her period declared her independent
i laughed out loud
just enough to feel the rumble in my tummy
but not to humiliate her
purity is no joke.
she prefers God over everything
gave herself away. daily.
and like clockwork she is renewed
we don't need to sound alarms or drive by with bullhorns
marching with placards
& chants about not going anywhere until freedom rings

B.Leah

SEXY

she never needed lingerie, a teddy,
or a little spray down there
from day one to forever
her sexy was wrapped in obedience
bending over backwards, her lips weren't pouty
she used them to birth nations
one. word. at. a. time.
she keeps him hoping with 3 words from the well
His water flows like streams beneath the surface
she really doesn't need anything at all
she chooses to go without the extra
hiding all her loveliness and he likes her there. uncovered.
a gift he doesn't need to unwrap
he'd been looking for her ever since he learned how to spell
T.H.E. C.H.R.I.S.T.
no difference between them, no rivers slicing them in two
one breath, one thought, one way
to keep them moving together
there's no time for hanging out on fences
make a choice, decide, & move on
we keep the conversation going well past the morning after
love making is beautiful
like God granting us new mercies - yesterdays aren't enough
so i will come home & never leave
i can grow our tomatoes from the window sill
i will learn how to sew and knit socks, we'll write textbooks
& i will show the children how to tie their shoes & to
reverence the Lord
i rather be so close. i can't see where you begin & i end
i want your boldness to rub off on me
like perfume on scarves
we left on the floor last night
you make me want to change my last name forever
no hyphens, no last name becoming part of my middle
going to city hall next week
i want to be Burgess until death rips me apart from you
you cover me in prayer & under blankets

so i can sleep warm
& you say I'm your gift
but i will not wait for you to ask me
on my knees begging
i don't need to be dignified
i could care less about what a woman is supposed to do or
not. i want to never be without your eyes
looking at me
i need you
to help me breathe.

©2015 B.Leah
"My Beloved & I"
Hartford, CT 2015

FATHER TIME

Somewhere between yesterday & the rapture
He looked her in the eyes & said "You are enough."
"they will probably tease, stare, and throw rocks but you are
a gem." Dad stands somewhere between 4'11 & 6'5
I'm not good with measurements,
Cuz He taught me how to love until the cup overflows
Heavier than he used to be, he carries patience and
gentleness. Loving his wife like Jesus loves us
They danced on rooftops, skipped stones every Sabbath
& made sure to bring cheerios to feed the trout
His voice carries his sons from disappointment to relief
Reaching in his pockets for knives to carve names in trees
He likes his fish broiled, his tea sweet, and clocks that tick
slow. He prefers to do the ironing, and then stands at a
distance to watch his wife. Her hips give birth to dreams and
sweet memories. Lips choosing to speak life & love - no sass
or shouts or ears ringing
She prefers submission over easy her father taught her well
"flip the eggs before they brown"

They are everywhere
Daddies in pews, picking up the left behind, running to catch
chickens, In school, debt free, in prisons, rehabs, in white
houses, Standing in pulpits, Sweeping streets nobody else
cares about Investing in children who haven't seen the light
of day, stringing kites, kissing boo-boo's & disciplining
children. We see you riding the bus arriving way before the
bell rings, Riding sanitation trucks & smiling wide like oceans
We see you on your knees, studying to show yourself
approved. Counseling children that lost their way,
greeting grown men with holy kisses
You're not afraid to hold your brother's hand, cry in public,
Or give the wrong answer. We see you burping babies
We hear you say "I. do." and mean it, fighting temptations
with God's word, We hear you speaking truth to power fists
in the air. Nothing but love pushing you to victory

We love your smile & your masculinity; we love your strength & your weakness. You keep it gangsta! Strapped with submission, letting go of pride. Your willingness to be vulnerable Is attractive. Your hands heal instead of harm, your eyes reassure; You make us feel safe at night and in the morning We want to greet you with grits & eggs - last night's meal will not do. You are dad & we love you, you are uncle & we cherish you. You are brother & we forgive you, you are friend & we need you. You are pop pop & we adore you. So ladies let's give a standing ovation for
Our dads, husbands, baby daddies, Uncles, pastor, elders, brothers. Respect and honor even when they don't deserve it
Soft answers keep arguments to a minimum

Dads we need your voice it helps us to find our way back
Back home, out of the dark, and away from danger
Making everything better than it was before
Dads we need your walk with Christ to be on point
No room for slacking or riding fences. Go hard or go home
Dads we need your love
Don't stop telling all of us that we are your favorite
Keep the gifts wrapped until we can open them
Keep your whole Armor on. We want to pick gentleness, joy, peace, patience, love, and self control

This is for you. Dads, soon to be dads, unmarried dads, Widower dads, Dads that do all the driving, dads that do all the cooking, men that father other people's children, Dads that can't see their children, dads who lost their children, dads that aren't respected, dads Who cry themselves to sleep at night, Dads that whisper prayers on the battlefields, dads who will never come home, Dads that don't pay child support, dads that pick up every weekend and drop off every Monday, Dads who are confused, mentally ill dads, dads with artificial limbs, dads who ride in chairs Everywhere they go, Dads we love you & we won't let you go!
Dad i love you & i won't let you go.

hunting season

i just want our sons to get old, wrinkly, eyes gon' blue
and hands popping with veins from hard work

i want them to bury their parents,
shop for maxi-pads once a month for their wives, shovel their walks,
take the garbage out, and get their mouths fitted for dentures

i want our daughters to live without being raped, sodomized,
abused in lit rooms unknowingly videotaped having sex,
deciding between stripping & porn

learning how to perform. fellatio, pole dancing, the art of seduction
from a sprite commercial or P.E.

i just want our daughters to be great grandmothers
in her 90's, waking up before sunrise, make their grand's oatmeal,
read the paper cut fresh dahlia's from her garden, harvest the tomatoes,

i need to calculate life

draw the value

on billboards

in textbooks

on TV. screens

and we all believe it.

takes courage

©2014 B.Leah
"Black Lives Matter Rally"
Hartford, CT

Use the space below to write your thoughts.
Write about the hopes and dreams you have for children.

LOVE

we never stopped being "the one". the sexual assault & cheating spouse. weren't deep enough to wash away beauty. the lies weren't bold enough to bury the story. we are still wonderfully made; even if we used to share our bodies with anybody who would pay attention. selling our dignity wrapped in crack cocaine. gunned down on Mather street. guns, violence & prostitution was not the end. we will live & not die. declaring how Great God is. we will cover each other in prayer. we will share a cup of sugar. and buy blankets for people sleeping under bridges. this is not the end. gangs are just groups of children that didn't get enough hugs. maybe they didn't hear the words "I'M HAPPY YOU ARE HERE TODAY". we all need to be cherished & wanted. in order to feel necessary. part of the equation & we have more than enough time. to speak to a child. long enough for them to start speaking back. don't you remember your surrogate parents? standing at bus stops, cleaning church pews, and collecting garbage. all of them shared the responsibility. clothing you in fearlessness. washing your face with boldness. whispering love in your spirit.

resistance is the power of letting go backsliding for excellence. like saying something when we need something. like looking for ways to reconcile with those who hurt us. i am not impressed with making folks feel guilty or inferior. just cuz' we don't speak the same language or can't walk without

help. i just want to see Thy Kingdom come in Hartford, Simsbury, and Bloomfield as it is in heaven. we are not exempt from digging deeper. when a young man or woman asks us for change. dimes
& quarters will never satisfy. we have to offer freedom at the cost of their faith and if they have none. use yours.

i'm sorry i don't have any goose bump filled love poems. Google can tell you the story of lovers walking on the beach. i want to talk about the Hope that sways from one side of the room to the next. i want to tell you about the Love that switches back & forth every time her hips roll. His footsteps tell the story about grace & mercy, and every time we seek the Father first He is pleased.

I want to tell you about love that never loses its flavor, it doesn't stop flowing because you're mad at each other. i want to tell you a story about staying until death parts you; no room for second chances or glances back at the woman in the café. i want to tell you about the fruit of the spirit and how you walk in the sanctuary and in your living room. i want to tell you about trusting the Father to pay your rent after your tithes. there is nothing sweeter than this, now & later and in between this & that, right after the fight.

but before you say I do, seek ye First the Kingdom of God & all these things will be given to you.

© 2015 B.Leah
"Reminder to Love"
Hartford, CT 2015

Use the space below to write your thoughts.
Write about your favorite things.

GET UP

She doesn't do easter

Or pastel baskets

Dyed eggs or bunnies

At least not altogether

She prefers pretty

Nails in feet

She doesn't hunt for treasures

And He rested after His work completed

He slept until it was time to Get Up

So   you   can   Get   Up.

ONE NIGHT STAND

In my opinion.

There is no such thing as one night stands.

The memory of Premarital Sex greets him at dawn

Every moan

There is no washing away

Hand prints on left cheeks

The hand meeting skin lasts until his last breath

Jesus forgives

But the taste in your mouth

You never forget

How it feels to wake up

Next to a stranger

Screaming inside

Cuz you did it again

Casual sex

Ain't like wearing jeans & jordans to church

It's like opening

The sweetest part of you

To the homeless guy with the sign that reads

"Will smash for food"

it's like tickling the inner thigh

Of the lady who squats and defecates in between bleachers

It's like giving birth vaginally on stage

At a gospel concert

Millions watching

Live and streaming and "youtubing"

Breech. Then emergency cesarean.

So before you nod upstairs, into laundry rooms,

Requesting boosts on top of speakers,

Being led to VIP booths dollars in hands

Paying for services that should never be on the menu

Be still. Be sure. & Brace yourself for the impact.

Jesus wants more for us

And the last time can be your last time

Until you say I do to the spouse of your prayers!

So before you kiss goodnight

Hoping to be swept off your feet

Be still and know that God is.

PRETTY LIES

She draws pretty lies

Wing tips on eyelids

contoured lips

& eyes made of bronze

reasons

and making more plans

to chisel & sculpt

masterpieces

& wanting to be better than before

in excellence

she sweeps bangs

behind ears

& waiting to be seen

without hands raised

singing louder and telling more

pretty lies

she shares pencils

and writes beautiful on eyelids

only she can see

lines & shapes

one size. fits beautifully

she jiggles in the middle

the only thing solid is her faith

wrapped in love

eyes & ears on the ground

ready to invest

she counts footsteps

& listens

SHE'S BLACK

do they know she's black?
like tar & feather, like Kush, like Nubia, like Togo
like Alabama, like north Philly, & Solomon's wife
like black, like struggles, and sit-in's, and conquering
and not letting go,
and dreams
do they know she's BLACK like us?
like Jesus
and renaissance,
and Hartford,
like Ferguson and fists
and panthers
like breakfast programs
and standing in lines to greet kings
like Garden & Mather,
like vine & Albany
like us, like wading in waters to deep
like reaching the shore in shackles, like being thrown
overboard
like throwing themselves overboard, like maafa
& big ol' bright teef smile,
do they know her thighs are black
like shaking hands every time they meet on treadmills &
runways
like "miss ceelie" black
do they know she got nappy hair?
do they know she black & beautiful
like the two is synonymous
like fish & grits,
Sabbath & rest,
fat & stretch marks,
man & wife
old & wrinkly,
today & tomorrow

do they know she's black & beautiful?

I WANT TO LOVE THEM

My seat is vacant
They prefer to sit together. Volume up. Right now.
Lecrae & Propaganda is the closest thing to the revolution
We are afraid of anger - so we wound & suffocate ourselves
And lie about Jesus.
Like He never turned tables over
In this temple we choose to experience it all
Joy. Sorrow. Trauma. Rage. Yes rage.
Like loud, fists clinched, molotov cocktails clinched between
our teeth
I want to love them beyond their racism & they are racist
It is absolute without feelings or remorse or systems of love
Bombs go off. my tongue bleeds Jesus & forgiveness
So we repeat until they hear us

We are valuable and I want to love you.
Like Yahweh taught us to rest on Shabbat & make
mountains shiver
I want to love them without reward of their smiley faces or
pink hearts
Or invitations to dinner or promotions

I want to love them even when they hate who I am.
But desire big lips, cushions in their panties, gentrifying our
menus
We pay to pick our movement. Charging us to recharge our
batteries.
Gentrification at its best popularizes the exodus of the poor
I wonder where they go from here
They want profit, cutting diamonds with their bare hands

I want to love them
This is by no means is easy
We are mostly human
So hatred & un-forgiveness comes easy

We hate our eyes & thighs & stretch marks
Of course there is room to hate each other
But I want to love them
    like running bath water
    like feed & clothe them
    like give them water when they thirst
    like running into fires to find them
I want to love them
    murders
    rapists & racists
    phony & hateful
    the one who stole his sons
    tax evaders
    white folks that tell you how to feel
    men that beat their wives or girlfriends
    cousins that molest their youngin's
    cheaters & liars
I want to love them

Use the space below to write your thoughts.
Write about the people that are hard to love in your world.

NO OUTLET

There is no outlet or walking or taking a break
or leaving each other behind.
This is it. The first & last time you say "i do"
In a gown & tux
With flower girls & best men
This is the challenge - to live until forever
Without letting go. For better or worse
When you get on each other's nerves or it's blissful
Everything between now & forever counts
Like coins in grandmom's change purse
Count every moment. Count every blessing.
Get lost in the treasures God blesses you with
Find each other in the dark & be the light
Season your love with salt until The Christ returns
You have been saying "I love you"
Don't stop the music that flows from your lips
We want to see you tomorrow and 80 years later
Playing the same song
No outlet when it gets to be more than you expected
No outlet after you've spent way beyond your means
No outlet in the middle of the argument
No outlet when you look at how much you have aged
No outlet. SHOUT it from Vine St. & Talcott Mountain
No outlet: your motto until death parts you
No outlet your prayer as you lay down to rest
No outlet until The Christ cracks the sky

©2014 B.Leah
"No Outlet"
Hartford, CT

Use the space below to write your thoughts.
Write about being separated.

INVESTMENT

I have a habit of talking
People down from cliffs
Away from fires & eventually she smiles
One day she'll know
How great she is
I chased her out of a burning building
She wanted to sit in the middle
Of the fire - roast s'more of her dreams
On skewers & pluck the annoying
Stubble from her chin
She never wanted to admit it
But she desired to love herself too.

How many times have you looked at yourself naked?
Turning to see your whole self and smiled
How many times have you opened your mouth?
And decided to take yourself seriously
How many times did you resist
        food, drugs, sex or cutting as comfort
Next time
Try Jesus.

SIDECHICKS

 i used to be her; on the side
chick waiting for phones to never ring
one time i ordered everything but the main dish
cornbread, sweet tea, greens, and potato salad
there will be no hands raised or clapped together
no fists - pumping pride and joy
no cheering or wishing to be more like chicks on the side
there is nothing romantic or sexy
being wanted so badly
by a man that didn't choose you
better yet that chooses to walk away from
covenants & favor
children & minds made up
he never wanted forever.
just today & tomorrow.
the revolution will be loved
and heard in the morning
when he calls to say "he's bringing you breakfast"
in bed is his motive
you on top
your love all sprawled out
gushing from ear to ear
giving him pleasure
meant for your husband
he will never leave for you.
his lies are pretty
when he spreads them over you
and tops it with diamonds, flowers, and trips to the zoo
holding hands
& saying forever
he will always forsake you.
he perjures himself daily
right hand on your breast
left fingers and toes crossed
his intention is to cut & divide you
leaving you barren
reserving his space

anytime it suits him
there is nothing romantic
about him calling you from the bathroom
or his car after drop off
if you listen closely
you can still hear his wife's last words
hanging on for dear life
hands clinched to bands
hoping he chooses marriage this time
they have children
he talks about them constantly
     he reminds you of how annoying his wife is
     rearranging your furniture
     he moves his stuff in by the carload
     so this is for women and girls
     who make choices
     with a sober mind
     forgiving themselves
     & doing 180 in the parking lot
     she calls freedom & forever
     by His first name
     Knowing Jesus will make it easier
     there is nothing easy
     about Sunday morning
     a week after you say goodbye
     body tingling
     memories of his touch
     alive like birds perched on window sills
     singing love songs
     you still hear his footsteps
     you thought the only thing that would stop you is death
     parting you
     & it did
     you dying to self for the first time
     was the best love story ever
     releasing your happy ending
     and letting God write a new story
     i hear your tears fall
     on pillowcases & shoulders

& your hands trembling
lonely is not the end
happiness is not the only tomorrow
there is more on the other side
whole & full
complete & together
& you will want to call him
just to say hello
you will want to see him
just to say goodbye
and it will feel like it's worth more
than a blood stained banner
& bigger than your piece of the pie

just wait.
till' morning

CHEERLEADERS

i just want to be your cheerleader
anytime you need a reason to not go back
every time you want to look in the mirror
demanding answers that no one can give
in the mornings when you wish you'd never met him
in the middle of the night when your legs quiver

i want to raise pompoms for you
and shout your name on top of mountains
and speak life into parts of you he killed
showing you - your face in the mirror
how fearfully & wonderfully made you are
how perfectly put together you are
naked. without the fluff
& this is the stuff our momma's didn't tell us about
the day after

it is hard to say goodbye to everything you owned
consumed in fires
you wish you died in
but today
we call you beautiful

©2015 B.Leah
Hartford, CT

RISE

she lay still longer than she could remember
hours, & days, & weeks
while the women gathered
her eyes wandering, irregular heart beats
replace patterns and traditions
of submission and obedience
she stopped recounting the trauma
long enough to light cigarettes
she forgot how to look up & above or beyond
her clothes are pretty
red bottoms & lashes daily
her wardrobe is endless
her lovers tell the world about the conquest
she stopped counting the number of times
she died, beaten, dehumanized and dismissed
lowered her price for services rendered
she knows how her feet look when she walks into
danger: eyes low, head bowed in shame
so we encourage her to
"Strip off your pretty clothes" & <u>RISE</u>
there is a place beyond her insecurities
a space reserved for the Master
if she listens. the hungry will eat
they will - walk
& the endangered and hunted
will be rescued
so "Strip off your pretty clothes" & <u>RISE</u>
there was no sense of urgency or victory or hope
her pockets full of comfort and pretty portraits
while other people's children lay dead in her front yard
shots rang - she pours another glass
wine helps her sleep through the trauma

she will never buy herself out of doubt or settling for comfort
but she tries daily
cash exchanging hands

she collects pocketbooks
she wears shackles like undergarments
holding her together
it's been a LOOOONG time
in this life, under the radar
giving up on everything
she settles for comfort
her lovers think she's sexy
she goes back for more
but i know God
who calls her from slumber
looking for water without a pale
He sees her. she's dying to be seen
struggling to be noticed
we just want more
like abundant & life and salvation
so we declare & decree "Strip off your pretty clothes" & RISE
we used to be her, clothed in linen
enough jewels to share
spent multiple decades collecting dust & jewels
her brooch budget is bigger
than my wedding
bands play her favorite song
she sends invitations to herself
she runs bath water
She tries to save herself
But I know God
loves her beyond
doubts, insecurities, and iniquity
i know God crushed death just for her. just for us.
we belong here. in the kingdom
holding her hand for lifetimes
she's better than she thinks
she's worth more than she believes
so we tell her again and again and again
"Strip off your pretty clothes" & RISE

© 2015 CAPTURED BY ELIJAH
WWW.CAPTUREDBYELIJAH.COM

ADORE

she would have picked blueberries
eating cheerios out of zip locks
counting her fingers to decide how many nickels she needed
buying her first pack of bubble gum
she would have sang
about lights shining bright
and not being afraid of the dark
she was going to echo prayers
in her sleep
dreaming of angels playing hopscotch
and saving children from brokenness
she would have had a PhD after her name
sharing theories
writing them into practice
investing in the city that tried to swallow her
declaring prosperity
in her parents health
she would have tied shoelaces
& painted boards on abandoned buildings
swept her front stoop
baked French toast & served it to her husband
counted her blessings
called her agent to request time away
sipping tea on back decks
wading in waters
smiling bright as the Son

but
it is finished
her breath
her heart. tiny. and precious.
stopped beating
during the beating.
so we say goodbye.

LUNCH BREAK

I will bring my leggings
Wear my sneakers
Tuck my earphones in my pocket
Move one foot in front of the other
I will not stop until the 60 is complete
I will enjoy
The fresh air
The daffodils bursting through frostbite
The green
The buds on trees
The birds that never stop singing
I will walk
For lunch
And eat at my desk
Greet you with hugs
And cheer you on
i will smile past you
And wave good-day
I plan to move well beyond 75 or 80
I want miles for lunch
And squats for dessert
Speaking things as though they already are
I will not stop after my first "huff"
& "puff" will not deter me
It's ok to be out of breath
While you walk away
Fries and donuts
Will not seduce me
We are not lovers
Or partners
Or friends
I will walk for lunch
Eat the sunlight
& drink the vine
Fully hydrated
& SATISFIED

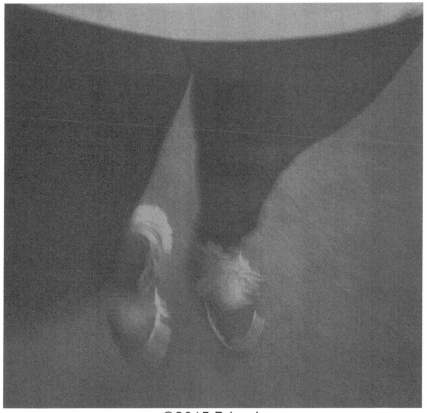

©2015 B.Leah
"Party time"
I like to call my walks during lunch a #lunchbreakparty)

Use the space below to write your thoughts.
Write about moving, movement, or movers.

PRETTY STRIKE

then they were distracted.
paying more for tension between thighs
pants tighter, waist trained, boots hugging, frames brighter
teeth whiter
they get dressed to tell a story of other people's property
they call home on their bodies
designed without you in mind
throwing parties imitating Christ's
first miracle
drunk without love
they carry girls & women upstairs into bathrooms
gang's run through them
taking trains. riding in shackles. fussing over lines
& poems they'll wear on dates
with other people's lovers
lips on gloss, batting eyes, battered thighs
coconut flour, confessions & brown sugar

now they drink milk & honey in the kingdom
awake & careless
crowns & jewels
abandoned dreams
satisfied
draped in salvation
no man can make or buy
we stand in doorways
picket signs & cheers
letting GOD make us pretty
backs swollen from praise
polishing shoes with skin cream
bucking systems
protesting fashion police
cutting hair against the grain
body on flawless
refocused
dreams colored with divinity

being better
than we look
refocused
restored
healed
and rejuvenated
content
& going without
The extras
make up
polish
or eyebrow maintenance

LETTING GOD MAKE US PRETTY.

SABBATH TRAIN

She misses her
More on the 7th
Than she does any other day
Sometimes she pretends to be sleeping
Hoping to catch a cold
So she can stay behind
Mother and daughter tight.
Like biscuits and syrup
She poured honey all over her face
Tears as sweet as sunshine and baby giraffes
"Tell me how you feel sugababy"
Alone
Nomadic
Disrupted
I want 5 on the pew
Or at least you
She used to Protest
Anti-going to church behavior
Making posters and looking for comrades
Her dolls all lined up
Ready to march
I prayed for a fighter
The girl that will stand up against all odds
And petition for her desires
A girl that looks in mirrors and tells herself
Sweet every things
Even when she doesn't feel pretty
A girl that wakes, prays
And starts the hash browns
Scrambling eggs
And steeping tea
On mom's day off
I couldn't be happier
She let me have it
Her good and sad
The bad and painful
There is more to living

Than Just breathing
It's best to fight
Fingers shaking
Heart beat speeding
Chasing fears away
And when you open your mouth to speak
The sun shakes it's tambourine
The birds sing you a special song
While we wait for you to come home

Use the space below to write your thoughts.
Do you know how to rest?

©2015 B.Leah
"sugababy & i"
HARTFORD, CT 2015

SIRENS

I have no plans
To get used to them
To welcome them inside after a long day
The sound of sirens
Calls attention to danger and regrets
Neglect and betrayal

We go running
To windows
And the block
The hood is always watching
Looking for misconduct
And tragedy
Some of us hear them daily
And is no longer a disturbance
The sound blends in with the birds chirping
People be screamin' at the top of their lungs
Fightin' for a dollar or their lives
It's all the same
I say a quick prayer for the living
Cuz the dead can't hear me - no way

I hope they do it too. hope
As wide as the sunrise
I HOPE THEY SEE ANOTHER & ANOTHER & ANOTHER

WERK

I wonder if she twerks for herself
Or does she report to a man,
her daddy is a boy
Making a life
Power & control is his currency

I want to throw rose petals at her feet
Welcome her
Hail her cabs in broad daylight

Her back is strong
Carrying men and women
Her dreams terrify her
So she stays awake
When his eyes are closed
She prays
And Fasts
Abstaining from white lines on Wednesday's
It is her only resistance

Until that great day.

#WOKEUPLIKETHIS

I wake up like this

Greedy

Prideful

Ready to swipe ideas and make them my own

i thank God, for Jesus.

Use the space below to write your thoughts.
What time did you wake up? What were your 1st thoughts?

NOTE TO SELF

when i eat like crap i feel like crap
eat like a human
when i eat like crap i feel like crap
eat like a human
when i eat like crap i feel like crap
eat like a human.

remember this feeling.
never forget.

Your Body is A Temple.
never forget.

You are priceless.
never forget.

Joy comes after the mourning.
never forget.

Use the space below to write your thoughts.
<u>Write a Note To Yourself.</u>

©2013 B.Leah
"Chicken & Journaling"
Manchester, CT

LOST 1's

if she never loses another pound
she would learn to cope with disappointment
she would be angry at first
she may feel worthless too
and will probably question her value
& ethic & determination & drive
she will deny gastric bypasses
& liposuctions & tucking tummies
she may even get depressed & not want to do anything
she would more than likely cry (like right now)
based on herstory she'd probably gain 5 or 50
she would not want to tell a soul
she'd reconsider every goal
she may want to give up everywhere
she wants to love herself as-is
she would learn to be content
she would question the desires of her heart
she would have to question her standards of beauty
she was introduced to her vanity
stared in that mirror for hours
she decided to wear a 2 piece

love & contentment.

if she never lost another pound she will have God.

if she never lost another pound she will have God.

if she never lost another pound she will have God.

if she never lost another pound she will have God.

if she never lost another pound she will have God.

if she never lost another pound she will have God.

if she never lost another pound she will have God.

FOR US

I know why God made us. For marriage.
I do - stretched out to forever
No place in time has recorded breath
Guinness cannot record
The number of times you look at me
And smile at the thought of your tears
When we said "yes"
Watches could not count how long it takes for me to release
My pride & say "yes"
I want to be yours beyond forever
I want to love you. long & sweet & full
With lips and eyes and my finger tips
Drawing hearts on your back
I would tattoo you to my eyelids
I want to see you in my dreams
And when I sneeze and especially when I yawn
I know why God made marriage. For us.
He wants us to bathe in each other's memories
Cleaning up all that we did before our eyes met
Coffee is sweeter when you brew it on top of forgiveness
In front of apologies and next to the love
Simmering near the Son
Light & clocks ticking
Counting down moments until I can say "yes" to you again
I want my body to say "yes" when you call my name
My lips to say "yes" when you require my attention
My posture echoes yes; defeating every no

Fear laid traps to deep to climb out
Defensive for no good reason
Deciding not to be open or available or loose or unlocked

That is until the Son said we were free
Free to be. Unfastened
Right in front of you

REBELLIONS

It is the moment you look
And you can't turn away
For the first time
You see
What God has always
And i want to live here forever
Fields of hope
Skyscrapers of love
Fruit from His vine
His kingdom on earth
A sip of heaven
In the middle of trauma And racism
She thought Wilson loved her
Gifts and special treatment

I hated to call him my grandfather
He pretended that mom-mom was dangling
from gym floors
Like bags waiting to be stuffed and punched
They tell me about my tears
When i was 2
He wanted suga'
I resisted
I've always been a rebel
Going against grains of injustice
I'd rather have quinoa and steel cut oats

We don't need the army to enlist us
We're already on the battle field

YESHUA

I need to stand on mountains, On chairs, or pews
And tell you about Jesus
That turned tables over, that came to divide "wanna-be's"
from disciples that resisted normative behavior. Jesus that
never lost sight of the real prize

You already know about Mangers, and stables, and virgins

I need to tell you about **The One**
Who won't back down; That sends us into battle against
giants with a slingshot and 5 smooth stones

I don't recognize this Jesus under trees and lights,
Pretty bows and candy canes

I need to tell you about Jesus
Who never lets us go
Who is coming back for His bride
And she has to stay ready and waiting for His return

So when the sky cracks
And we all see what we've been hoping for
It will be too late to repent or forgive
So do it now.
It will be too late to reconcile and love enemies
Drop everything. Go now. Seek forgiveness. Reconcile with
your neighbor.
Clear the air. Confess your faults to the Lord. Seek
resolution.
Find your dysfunctional parent and honor them. Repent!
Stop fornicating, lying and cheating on your spouse.
End your relationship with your addictions.

Stay ready to receive the King.
Unpack your bags and Release your hurt.
And stay ready.

Dear you,

It takes a lot of strength, grace, desire, hope, faith, and love to get up every day and do what you are assigned to do. The number of times you thought you would lose, die, or not come back to a sense of normalcy is astronomical! But you did or are on your way back!

There is nothing more attractive than you defying the odds, never letting go, or deciding to never look back! Your decision to eat healthier, to exercise regularly, quit smoking, or risk it all and leave that abusive relationship is the definition of taking courage!

I know you've thought about giving up. Ending it all. Or going back to the way things used to be. The way you used to be was for that season in your life. Those former coping skills (mediocrity, laziness, casual sexual relationships, behaving like a slave...) will not work now.

I encourage you to dig deep, cry loudly, grunt if you have to but keep moving forward. This life #takescourage and my friend you have it!

Use the space below to write your thoughts. <u>What courageous thing will you do today?</u>

The center of courage is love. Dive into God's never ending bank of love. It is this love that rewards us with courage to take with us on our journeys!

#TakesCourage

ABOUT THE AUTHOR

B. Leah is a wife, mother, friend, victim advocate, a firebrand Spoken Word Artist, Co-Founder of Outta Da Box Ministry and a disciple of Christ. For as long as B.Leah can remember she followed crowds and other folk's dreams. At 37 years old she will return to the academy to follow her prayers and God's plan for her life. She is going back to college to earn her Master's & Doctorate degrees in order to provide non-traditional and creative therapeutic support for survivors of emotional trauma in urban spaces.

B. Leah as a Poet & Spoken Word Artist has used her voice to dare audiences to hope in the midst of emotional tsunamis. She was a member of The CT Poetry Slam Team (2001) and The Bulanians (2001-2003). Her work has been documented in her first chapbook "Evolutions of Revolutionary Tactics", 'The Thick Chronicles" a stage play about healthy body image, and several online blogs and magazines. A friend wrote "your life is your testimony, and these poems bear witness!!!"

Degrees and honors are great expressions of what she does. But who she is alone standing in the mirror is most important. B.*Leah is available to speak and share poetry at your wedding, events, special ceremonies, convocations, and memorial services/funerals. For more information please contact iambleah1@gmail.com or (508) 622-5324.*